Encyclopaedia
Chloe Elliott

NEWPOETSLIST

the poetry business

Published 2023 by
New Poets List
The Poetry Business
Campo House,
54 Campo Lane,
Sheffield S1 2EG

Copyright © Chloe Elliott 2023
All Rights Reserved

ISBN 978-1-914914-53-9
eBook ISBN 978-1-914914-54-6
Typeset by Utter
Cover image: Marissa Rodriguez on Unsplash
Printed by Biddles Books

Smith|Doorstop Books are a member of Inpress:
www.inpressbooks.co.uk

Distributed by NBN International, 1 Deltic Avenue,
Rooksley, Milton Keynes MK13 8LD

The Poetry Business gratefully acknowledges
the support of Arts Council England.

Contents

5	Aupair
6	Body
7	Cow
10	Dreamtheory
11	Eating Orange Peel Is An Act Against God
12	Encyclopaedia
13	Fishcoarse
14	Gay Club
15	Grey Pennant
16	Lacan's Ladies
17	Leotard
18	Red Is The Body Electric
21	Sever
22	Tripe
23	Ungracious
24	Wasps
25	Water
26	Acknowledgements

The emperor was a fickle god.
He preferred to be thrilled by an automatic bird

in filigreed gold. A musicbox, a leitmotif.
Love me, please. Orange blossom.

– Sarah Howe, 'A Certain Chinese Encyclopaedia'.

Aupair

And then the kid makes a joke about a pointy hat & says your trousers would fit in a paddy field. And then he says god won't deliver you quick into kindness and you don't hold anything extraneous or even qualify with the parts that count, the parts that will get you through the golden gates and past the undulating men who resemble Peter Sarsgaard. And then his dad is looking at you in a funny kind of way at dinner. Touching your feet. I say *fuck you, fuck you Benedetto, I'll spit gluten into your polenta, that'll show you my good heart and my teeth that break at this time of month.* Anyway, he was only eight so I didn't do any of that and just asked for it with milk instead.

Body

Hello again old friend hello furuncle old tired spaceship that
sometimes struggles to make it in the morning struggles
to wake   let me hold your hand what will come away if not
the beeswax and thread the yarn for the French folds
and gaps in the bind   the secret pockets that carry chopped
thumbs cherry tomatoes and train tickets   let's try rolling
you out until you resemble a Helen Frankenthaler
be a girl who is all for experiments   reach into yourself
and find a paste that is strict and fractious the sting
of sunburn and consistency of sambal belachan
          pull that stuff out   live your new dreamlife as
a puddle of goop   a damp sheet of dough unsuitable
for lasagne but perfect for heavy clay & rose growing

I'm saying squeeze yourself between the stones of an aluminium
printing press and lie back. Pretend you're on a beach in Viareggio.
The soft whir of the waves as Rilke strokes the moles on your back.

Cow
After Blast Beach and the Tarot of Marseilles

III

We go searching for the cows, for their black
belted bodies. We find the Empress in the field,
woman of no longing. White ribbon splices open
her turnball coat like a harpoon through a whale.
I am a daughter of doubt, don't believe Tommy
when he says the sea is over there, make no notice
of the blue that degrades into larger, deeper blue.
But it does, farmers scythe the land, bodies grow
in mildew, we shuffle the cards.

XIV

Dragonfly wings butter in the sun
like smoked herring. The slickness of the day
catches at an angel's halo. It's hot enough
to persuade the angel to slip out of her wings,
those two halves of an auburn heart matted
like a pheasant. She slips out of her deck
and leads us to a red bridge over a coastal train track.
Uses shells to make crucifixions at the bits in her legs
she hates, carving out skin like spouts of a strawberry planter.
The coves stretch out like great labyrinths,
their slick bellies baking in salt and algae.
Belts of seaweed scream like the mangled pipes
of a choral organ. She doesn't make a big deal
out of it but she's got a choice to make.

X

Tommy's telling me how as a child his father would
get him to carry beechwood. Broad flat planks curved
like a muscle, kind enough to be stacked into dens
or barbecue grills. His father once dived into a rockpool
fully clothed to fetch him out. Dropped out of art college
and made all the National Trust designs, stole engines, dealt
cranberry glass and then stopped for the good pots and sweet babies.
Tommy cooks too many mushrooms and his coats always
smell of weed but he's got an angel on his chest and
a dove on his shoulder. Soft hands and dark brown eyes
like a boy I once knew in Tuscany. I'd give him the Priest,
the Lovers, the Wheel. I'd give him a field of terracotta statues,
eyeholes cinched with pencils. I'd give every smack
and sunny blunt of the Apollo and then a heart that matched.
An orange satin dress wet in the rain. I'd walk into the waves
and fish him out with the whelk and the worst parts of ourselves.
There's so many things I'm hiding behind. But the sea was there
the whole time – the hard tortoiseshells in their pelts telling us to choose,
the backs of belted Galloways like two right-winged angels,
the great heaving strapped to the sky.

Dreamtheory

I am fearing my own coldness, I mean the parts
of myself that are resolute, are hovering inside
of me like plasma. Derrida says infinite alterity,
the completely other, the dead, living in us.
Like issues of chia seed. Ghostly cell walls,
translucent to the point of purple, a fraction
I cannot cross. I can't begin again.
I'm so sick of newness. Give me the beehive,
the piecebag, the quilt. I carry you with me
wherever I go.

Eating Orange Peel Is An Act Against God

the sand tells me, and I laugh. Look here buddy; this mandarin sits different. Inside this mandarin is a small Chinese girl curled up with toes that aren't yet toes but clusters of milkweed. Let me tell you how to make a mandarin like this. She should only be cut open with a palette knife, see, you have to spin her like skinning a snapper, keep her turning on the balls of your fingers until she grows bigger and bigger and dizzy until she splits. Then you can bleed her but wear marigolds in case she spills. The milk's a cardenolide, pink like a nightslip or a darling's foam and toxic if consumed in large quantities. You know when it dries, it crusts over like amber and makes a seal, or seven or eight of them. these words spoken in season. If you pluck them individually and lay them in the palm of your hand you can see them beating. Small white roots tapping on a Georgian window as the sun sets. They leave trails like drawings on a shower door the way the heat will permit. Where the tiles repeat back the afternoon to a room that is ochre is boneyard is everything waiting to be sunken or read to or made a malt drink. If you line the girls up they spoon each other like kidney dishes and in each kidney dish is a kidney that if pieced together will make the bisection of a rose; a stained glass wheel. The crown of a saint's head peeping through a loft hatch. in every segment there is a kneeling; a stubborn vesper.

As you prepare the knife the windows begin to rattle and then her shoulders. They pucker in Droste effect.

Encyclopaedia

The sad drooping cow is in the corner. She's resting on a wreath of blue tiles, doing her best to look up all these words. Drawing at plumes beneath the host's feet. Holding a drumstick that draws out into a falchion, the one that slays the Emperor and gets you free wine at the house party. She finds herself as a dissolving cork and a roulette wheel that tastes like peaches. She's drowning in the index and is confused by the reference system. Who uses MHRA anyway? At the party she bumps into her landlord and asks about the extractor fan, asks what it means to lead someone through a river. The filter's all clogged up. What does it mean to all those horses in all those Ada Limón poems?

They do it with such ease; they bend their knees, pay their rent, take a disassociating side step. Tradition does its best to get on its front but is never centrally loaded. The horses emigrated to Sardinia when they predicted Tesco would go that way. They're good at being mixed, the Friesians and the Appaloosas. The sad drooping cow has decided on vellum, decided she is going to start a scrapbook where all the animals look at each other. Cut up the coastlines so Marsden Rock silts into the West Coast. Make them hold hooves and montage their frames in black and white stilts so it looks like they're all alive at once. She wants to carry light the way they can, splitting the load between the mares, stamping their skinny ankles in the eddies.

Fishcoarse

On the train I am explaining how an orgasm is the moment
when you can't see the fish but you know they are there because
of the ripples radiating outwards. Against a blue plastic seat
you wriggle in weariness and I think of the little grottos we have
made that morning. You say *show me* so I paint the bed in UV;
pronouncing this is how I see the world, the whole coarseness coming apart
in sandy fistfuls of electric green. I couldn't be white even if I tried.
Each stained finger, mouth and grossness; each whisker like
a fluorescent glowstick. I'm saying it's like a fish taking a series
of breaths, rising to the surface as they break the tension on water.
The carp I saw on the sleepers was a fox all along.
The track is stained, is easing out of itself, releasing a stream
of fallen leaves and Portuguese millipedes whilst the carriage shakes,
hot and drenched in urine, like an infinity room that cannot stand
to touch itself. Here is the difference, the signifier between lack and lack.

Gay Club

Adrian glowed that evening, had glow worms underneath his cheeks,
when he held them up to the lamplight he saw them wriggle,
saw them like the inside of a marble, like hot glass being blown,
saw the punty inoculate the night, saw my cells dancing. He wanted
never to wear matching socks, thought thumbs should never exist,
imagined every body as a boulder and asked them to move really
kindly. You don't understand how long we had to stand in that queue,
how when we left they were still in line, a purple garland that unfurled
into the Wear. He'll turn his lava lamp off this time. We'll make our own jazz bar.
It'll be jazz every day, not just on Mondays and no one will push you
down the stairs. There will be enough space for all the jazz enthusiasts,
in fact, they'll get melon on arrival. We'll make the whole thing out of
whalebone and Chinese karaoke and we'll serve espresso martinis in
petri-glasses sealed with algal bloom and how Mina Loy will laugh,
how she'll still life us with our pink coughs and white rabbit hearts.

Grey Pennant
As taken from Dulux Paint

Speaks easy. Vomits up love, that pigeon wing cootie catcher. How easy – run of garlic like a spat-out oyster on bruschetta. I snap the necks of all the men in my life and they fizz. Fluster out like the sprinklers turning on. Cement hardens underwater if undisturbed but I spill onto the caulking until the bath leaks. This grey fracturing. These double corniche ceilings sad without restraint. Build an aqueduct with volcanic ash. Tip it in loose and it all blows away. Blow up love, that clamshell grey pennant. Dull coin of fortune, always landing tails, all decisions (life, love, career) made as a marker of this. Always the wrong one, but, hey, you committed. It'd be embarrassing not to go ahead now. Make a life like this. Make it highly pozzolanic. Swap the weeks of all the moons. Buy razor blade packets. Sweep lime powder off the edges of the sink.

Lacan's Ladies

At Herne Hill station the sex has gone nothing like
the first time but there's celery growing out of a planter
that reads HAVE A NICE DAY
in rickety black paint and I see a couple split as one
morphs into a suit and runs to a bathroom as a nun.
I don't see it but I imagine her vomiting a collection of dice.
On platform two is a giant carp thick and exhausted
with the weight of itself as it buries into the track, its belly
a wet chiaroscuro that rustles against the hedge.
When it writhes, a series of tunnels pass through its coat,
shuddering like a hellmouth that collapses into a small black slug.
Growing out of focus like the body that wraps herself in sheets and
rolls away. Before it disappears, the carp croons the house of the rising sun
and the rush crowd repeat back, blowing a series of *o's*
as their morning cheerios spill orange onto the track.
Meanwhile I am here persevering. I am asking you to see me.
Pressed against the window, taking these three or four breaths.

Leotard

I am a small parcel   a small peach in a brown paper bag
a tightly cornered hot-crossed bun   I tremble in a tin
I love Victorian buildings   I fall asleep in a red renault cleo
am so kind   am so tired   go for the bread at Christmas
and wait by the indicator chasing drops in the windows
making the crumb moist I stick the whitest part up my nose
the body of Christ in bits   when I get there I don't want to
paint tears   point toes or plié in the mirror but I stage myself in fourth
these days I will point my toes in the shower or walking
or when he pins my legs in the air   there something in me straightens
though never total he kisses my calves and I gesture fondness
for the tautness of shoes   the pink leather like a skinned pig
without the requirement for dye   they'll call my name but I am pain
fully shy I can't go   I don't go up to collect the award

Red Is The Body Electric

I

Mother maxes out on the epidural. Sucked out with a vacuum,
six pounds falls out like a jaundiced pup. The nurse thrusts a pink
lettuce leaf toward a matsaleh as she declares *looks like the father*.

II

When you buy the morning after pill
in Italy there is no consultation or white room
in the back. No pharmacist asking
when your last period was
and if condoms are really working
or have you thought about the pill or coil
but instead you type the night before
into google translate. You tap out the text
pillola del giorno dopo per favore onto
your white screen like frosting a pillar of salt
and then slip a pink cube under your tongue,
chasing it up with a cappuccino.

For the rest of the day, the lower half
of your body peaches in splits.
When you want to calm yourself
you think of every part inside disassembling
and you imagine your liver and abdominal cavity
uncoupling like a giant jigsaw.
Shaking hands and walking away
in the rain, no phone numbers exchanged,
just revisiting moments of the conversation
on the walk home.

III

An ex hears Mum on the phone
and laughs when she pronounces *three*.
When I am five, Hasti has a nosebleed.
Mother sits me down and forces me to memorise
the shape of English coins. Two pence thin and flat
like a radish, fifty like a flowered mooncake.
When I place my thumb, index and middle finger
together to make a parsed tongue, she scolds me,
says *there is no such thing as three pee,*
they will call you stupid if you say that.
Hasti is still upside down with a wad of tissue,
dredging the rosiest parts.

IIII

My period comes on Valentine's Day, two weeks late. I took
a pregnancy test but forgot to use a morning sample, thereby
jeopardising the result. I ask someone to get a pack of paper strips. *But*
why do you need five? You never know. I imagine myself being pregnant
five times. The double red strokes appearing thick and squat. I leave the
test on the rim of the bath, the watery yellow mixing and unspelling
the pigment. I want to carry all the blues inside me like splitting oil. If I
had five pregnancy sticks I would have also had four abortions. Which
could be four doses of mifepristone and four doses of misoprostol or
four instances of vacuum aspiration, each lasting ten minutes. Or I
could have done both the pills and surgery, breaking my lining down
like tearing tinfoil. Of all the things I carry inside me, this is the worst.

IIII

Valentine's Day lands in the same month of sad,
falling two weeks after Chinese New Year.
The angpao reds carried forward, two oceans away.
I am not at home for either holiday and neither is Mum.
I say *gong xi fa cai* though search it beforehand
to doublecheck the spelling. I ask her if she's doing
anything and she doesn't reply, though texts a photo
of a clubcard voucher and a Google internship. *You don't
need a degree to work at Google, they train you and you
can work from home.* I go to Chinatown in Newcastle
and though all the Malaysian cafes are booked out
pick the busiest looking restaurant with space.
When ordering, I ask for a surprise, though really
meaning a blue plate of duck rice. Forty minutes later,
a circular platter emerges with ice, yellow flowers,
and flanks of salmon. In the middle is a pool of rose petals,
white at the base, blushing towards the tip.
Clam, the waitress declares, *my favourite*.
Gummy and tasteless in my mouth, I swallow and smile
at her dutifully. She is Chinese with a Glaswegian accent
and I wonder if she too is surprised when I speak.
She places a wad of cardboard underneath the table to steady it
and suddenly a part of me wants to hold her, bury my face in her hair.
Tell her I walked the whole of Tyneside for a pomelo.
Recount that in the body electric, those parts most ruined
will fizz like expired melon. That out here the permission
to locate a bleed is never signed. We do our own surgeries,
our own hash jobs, gesticulating and cleaving in the dark.
Look how good we're getting at shucking these bodies.
Look at the clams that spill open from their filmy shells.
We, who are so lost, so out of love, choosing cruelty
over language, stacking plates, collecting knives.

Sever

Moon scallop in a pan.
I scythe a thumb, watch it squid
and slip down the drain with the hair dye
and goldfish. I fold a perfect circle,
a dazzling pearl for a perfect boy.
Only meaning to cut
a straight line for an apology but
slipping quick with a boxcutter
and a plastic ruler. Scalpel
slipping off the paper like a suit
of dalmations. Lying in hospital
whilst something purple on my neck forms,
ruling out pianos and conscription
and becoming an astronaut.
I propose with the best
part of myself wrapped in tissue.
In the cold sticking out like a sore whelk.
The albumen spilling out alongside the ladybirds.
Everyone tries to climb back
into their body but what's the point?
I go oyster harvesting like the rest of you.
Eat wet steak and press doorbells and peel eggs.
I win every thumb war all the same.
I can carry a gassy toast and jump off egg rock
singing glorious glorious
extravagant, thinking this must be what love is like,
thinking fuck the stitches,
I'm going to bellow from the rooftops
and not care where my red heart lands.

Tripe

Well it's louder than you think like the bone
fragments of a gutted conch not like congee
but it cleaves the same like entering a cherry orchard
in autumn seeing all the birds suckling chee cheung fun
on the floor outside the cathedral chewing berry wholeness
smacking gum like atomic bombs whilst the priests
greet every ghost with ruffled collars of silk
like a magician asking you to spin into his arms
as you hold the card in your mouth the sharpie
and illusion sharpening on your tongue the red heart
of a quill pig inverted all the needles facing in
producing a coat of just buccal mucosa the best way
is in honeycomb or at a cricketmatch on a long piece
of flatbread oh it was absolute heaven I'll say

Ungracious

Orange blossom slips off the knife in rings of white –
the leaves crushed with a flat blade make for a tambourine
devout to chilli powder & soft & flakes & thick & banana & leaves
& how do I gesture back to the small boy that I too am alive
& hurting & forgetful of language
I am in the eddies in a waxy noose unable to foster newness
unable to call this home unable to name flowers but here I go

Wasps
After Patrick White

A great slab of marble at the weight of three great men divided the room. As she spoke over him the dog saw the little whites of the Italian man's eyes and the mean meat of his teeth like peeled crawfish as they kissed his mouth. Now they sucked making a tsss sound. Now the woman had finished and the man let her and he paused as if he was being handed a stranger's coat, having to go to great lengths not to crease it. He fixed out the collars before hanging it on the rack. *Ah, I remember what I was saying now*, he said. And then resumed for the silence had been dragged out enough, had been whittled into a thin bone, heavy enough to punish her. He resumed, deliberately and in impression, flicking the heads off the words as he blew them out. They would grow bigger and bigger, threatening to gorge the clouds above the dog and the kitchen. A paper lantern, the kind for a burial decoration, though purposed for Carnevale, the dog observed, had just passed in and out of the skylight. It was a flap he could not ripple through. Ultimately it would never reach full height because wool is the least to burn and so the words sank into the concrete floor and slivered and folded in on themselves as all bodies of shame must do. So the conversation continued and the light was put out like flattening wasps. All because the couple's fingers were wet every time they went to press the flame.

Water

I swim in you once in Greece. In green summer algae,
where underneath everything looks to be strung up. I dreamed all of this,
dreamed we hung our ears up in the Aegean Sea like a series of wet postcards.
I know little about encyclopaedias, least of all how to spell them
but I know we opened one underwater. The categories splitting open
like the ribs of an angel. I'll rent a bassinet for bible paper and hanker
for a better bestiary but my body has changed. My handwriting is looser,
leaves more space for the innumerable parts that don't join like they used to.
Like larvae carried about the room to breathe, I see the dip dip dip of a fish
that abides the lifelines of a circular body. And how the water makes us
like children's drawings. Blurs us so we are slow and fabulous,
so we take too much time to be dedicated fingers. But we definitely have souls,
each piece like an octopus' sucker, a blue tealight plastered over a sheet.
The whole batch as blue as telling someone you love them in an aquarium,
as the fish come up to the glass and blow crenelated kisses.

The y as beautiful as a candied cherry stem, leaping off the dock
into symmetry as it absolves, worrying you for a second as it leans back.

Acknowledgements

'Gay Club' first appeared in Issue 68 of *The North* and 'Grey Pennant' in *Ink Sweat & Tears*. 'Eating Orange Peel Is An Act Against God' is the Gold Winner of the 2020 Creative Futures Award and has been published by Bad Betty in *Field Notes on Survival*.

I would like to thank Kym Deyn, Steve Dearden, Fahad Al-Amoudi, Malika Booker, Denise Saul and Sam Riviere for their feedback, support and mentorship. To Rachel Long – many of the poems that appear in this book, including the title, emerge from a fantastic Poetry School freewrite. A massive thank you is owed to Jenny Danes for her kindness and effervescence, for holding and bringing into reality the first edition of this pamphlet. To my family and friends and of course to Maddy, Adrian and Andy, who many a time have laid beside me as I read them these poems.